Acknowledgement of Land & of the Traditional Owners of this Land

I would like to acknowledge the Gadigal people of the Eora Nation, upon whose stolen land I stand on today.
I recognise that this land was never terra nullius — the land belonging to these peoples was never ceded, given up, bought or sold.
I would like to pay my respects to Aboriginal Elders past, present and emerging, and I extend this acknowledgement to all Aboriginal and Torres Strait Islander people.

This book is dedicated to all the "ALIENS" out there!
You know who you are!

-"The Don"
08.03.2021

Foreword

Vito, what can I say?

You ever had a bad day?
The Sun leads your way.
Life is fun when its play.
All we really have is today.
We say hello almost every day.

Energy is real and you are electric to those who you love and your community.
Press on.
Live on.
Be strong.
For it won't be long.
Till we are all six feet under.
Such is life.
What a wonder.
Thank you for your friendship, my brother.

Ali
07.03.2021

Contents

1: Accept that you are Alone
(Accetta di Essere Solo)
2: Domestic Partnership
(Convivenza Domestiche)
3: When She's Made Up Her Mind
(Quando ha Deciso)
4: Everyone Needs Someone to Play With
(Tutti Hanno Bisogno di Qualcuno con cui Giocare)
5: Relationships
(Relazioni)
6: The Potato Wars
(Le Guerre delle Patate)
7: I Wanna Make Lo♥e WITH You
(Voglio Fare l'Amore Con Te)
8: A Stolen Kiss
(Un Bacio Rubato)
9: Friendship Vs Relationship
(Amicizia Vs Relazione)
10: There's Nothing More to Say
(Non c'è Altro da Dire)
11: Comfortable in Your Own Skin
(Comodo Nella tua Pelle)
12: It's All in Your Mind
(È Tutto Nella tua Testa)
13: Life Is Not Meant to Be So Complicated
(La Vita non Dovrebbe essere così Complicata)
14: The War to End All Wars
(La Guerra per porre Fine a tutte le Guerre)
15: You Didn't Even Stop to Say Hello
(Non ti sei Nemmeno Fermato a Salutare)
16: Party Animal
(Festaiolo)
17: You Must Play Hard to Get!
(Devi Giocare Duro per Ottenere!)

Contents

18: Create a Vacuum
(Crea un vuoto)
19: The Life of an Idiot
(La Vita di un Idioto)
20: Cunt (is not a dirty word)
Fica (non è una sporca parola)
21: Everybody's So Fucking Boring
(Sono tutti così Fottutamente Noiosi)
22: The waiting Game
(Il Gioco in Attesa)
23: Nothing Ever Happens the Way You Want It To
(Non Succede Mai Niente nel Modo in cui lo Desideri)
24: I Know Nothing
(Io non so Nulla)
25: Honesty is the Best Policy
(L'onestà è la Miglior Politica)
26: Partners in Crime
(Complici nel Crimine)
26: You Talk a Lot for Someone with Nothing to Say
(Parli Molto per Qualcuno che non ha Niente da Dire)
27: Birthday
(Compleanno)
28: Throw Caution to the Wind
(Getta Cautela al Vento)
29: You Can't Be Everything to One Person
(Non Puoi essere tutto per una Persona)
30: People Take Life Too Seriously
(Le Persone Prendono la Vita Troppo sul Serio)
31: Empty Chair
(Sedia Vuota)
32: I Am TOO Loud
(Sono TROPPO Rumoroso)
33: I Can Be Quiet
(Posso Stare Tranquillo)

Contents

34: Time Heals All Wounds
(Il Tempo Guarisce Tutte le Ferite)
35: My World
(Il Mio Mondo)
36: Time
(Tempo)
37: Use It or Lose it
(Usalo o Perdi)
38: Tinder Surprise (Kinder for Adults)
Tinder Surprise (Kinder per Adulti)
39: Everything Has A Price
(You're gonna have to pay somebody!)
40: Power is Evil
(Il Potere è Male)
41: Time Heals All Wounds (Hurt)
(Il Tempo Guarisce tutte le Ferite (Ferite))
42: Doing Nothing is the Hardest Thing to Do
(Non Fare Nulla è la Cosa Più Difficile da Fare)
43: Soulmate (& Myself)
Anima Gemella (e Me Stesso)
44: Energy
(Energia)
45: Don't Get Married
(Non Sposarti)
46: Born to DIE!
(Nato per Morire!)
47: You're Having TOO MUCH FUN!!
(Ti Stai Divertendo TROPPO !!)
48: I'm Selfish
(Io sono Egoisto)
49: I Stared into the Faces of Death
(Fissai i Facce della Morte)
50: The Club of Rome
(Il Club di Roma)

Accept that you are Alone
(Accetta di Essere Solo)

You are born alone.
You live alone.

You are alone.
With your family, you are alone.
In a marriage, you are alone.
In a partnership, you are alone.
In a crowd, you are alone.
When you hold someone, you are alone.
When you hug someone, you are alone.
When you kiss someone, you are alone.
When you go to sleep with someone, you are alone.
When you are fucking someone, you are alone.
Even when making LO♥E, you are alone.
When you die, you are alone.
You are ALWAYS alone.

Alone you are born.
Alone you live.
Alone you die.
You are ALWAYS alone.

Accept, that you are ALWAYS alone.
And you will NEVER be alone anymore!

"The Don"
06.11.2020

Domestic Partnership
(Convivenza Domestiche)

Domestic arrangement.
Friends without benefits.
Co-habitation.
Mutually beneficial.
Comfortable existence.
Everyone's a winner.
It's a "win-win Situation".

There's one thing missing though.
In this "blissful co-habitation".
This cosy domestic arrangement.
This neatly packaged situation.
And that is PASSION.

There is no "vim" or vigour".
There is no "Fire in the belly".
There is no "Heat between your loins".
There is no DESIRE or infatuation.
There is no "long lasting looks".
There is, no "furtive sideways glances".
There is no "dry lips & dry mouth".
There is no "lump in my throat".
There is no "boner in my pants".

But it's not a bad situation.
It serves i's purpose.
It's comfortable for everyone.
It's easy & it works.
So, why "rock the boat"?
Why create an unhappy situation.
Just "let it be".
That's what I say.
"If it ain't, broke why fix or tamper with it"?

There are far worse situations to be in!

"The Don"
07.11.2020

When She's Made Up Her Mind
(Quando ha Deciso)

There's no stopping her.
When she's made up her mind.

There's nothing you can say.
When she's made up her mind.

There's nothing you can do.
When she's made up her mind.

There's no turning back.
When she's made up her mind.

There's no argument you can make.
When she's made up her mind.

She knows just what to do.
When she's made up her mind.

She knows just what she wants.
When she's made up her mind.

She knows just what it takes.
When she's made up her mind.

There ain't no turning back.
When she's made up her mind.

She's a "hard-headed woman"
When she's made up her mind.

There ain't no turning back.
When she's made up her mind.

She always stays on one track.
When she's made up her mind.

She ain't gonna change her mind.
When she's made up her mind.

She never ever, even looks back.
When she's made up her mind.

"The Don"
07.08.2020

Everyone Needs Someone to Play With

(Tutti Hanno Bisogno di Qualcuno con cui Giocare)

Everyone needs a playmate.
Everyone needs a play friend.
No matter how young.
No matter how old.

Someone you can have fun with.
Someone you can be crazy with.
Someone you can let your hair down with.
Someone you can sing with.
Someone you can dance with.
Someone you can do dumb things with.
Someone who will let you be "stoopid".
Someone you can make LO♥E with.

Just like when we were kids.
With no responsibilities.
With not a care in the world.
Where we were free to do whatever the fuck we liked.
Do whatever the fuck we wanted to.
Go wherever the fuck we wanted to.
Stay up all night if we wanted to.
Drink & smoke as much as we liked.

All night, if we wanted to.
And into the next day,
If we wanted too.
Just "hanging", was never a problem.
We had all the time we wanted!
We were in no hurry to do anything.

So, everyone needs someone to play with.
Those days are not dead & buried.
Have fun today.
Don't think about tomorrow.
Loosen up.
Chill out!

Find someone to play with.
I know that they are not that easy to find.
In this world full of anger & hatred.
But you need to, for your own "state of mind"!
Because everyone needs someone to play with.

Just like we used to.
All those years ago.

"The Don"
07.11.2020

Relationships

(Relazioni)

Relationships should be *fun*.
Relationships should be *enjoyable*.
Relationships should be *pleasurable*.
Relationships should be *desirable*.
Relationships should be *passionate*.
Relationships should be *joyful*.
Relationships should be *playful*.
Relationships should be *light*.
Relationships should be *wonderful*.
Relationships should be *energetic*.
Relationships should be *energising*.
Relationships should be *comfortable*.
Relationships should be *relaxing*.
Relationships should be *relaxed*.
Relationships should be *happy*.
Relationships should be *peaceful*.
Relationships should be *warm*.
Relationships should be *intimate*.
Relationships should be *personal*.
Relationships should be *safe*.
Relationships should be *cosy*.
Relationships should be *protecting*.
Relationships should be *nurturing*.
Relationships should be *creative*.
Relationships should be *magical*.
Relationships should be *mystical*.
Relationships should be *spiritual*.
Relationships should be *soulful*.
Relationships should be *musical*.
Relationships should be *He♥rtfelt*.
Relationships should be *Lo♥ing*.
Relationships should be *easy*.

How are your relationships?

"The Don"
08.11.2020

The Potato Wars

(Le Guerre delle Patate)

The Food Wars.
The Energy Wars.
The Space Wars.
The Sexual Wars.
The Financial Wars.
The Opium Wars.
The Cannabis Wars.
The Drugs Wars.
The Religious Wars.
The Mind Wars.
The Mindless Wars
The Nuclear Wars.
The Political Wars.
The Arms Wars.
The Crazy Wars.
The Insane Wars.
The Intellectual Wars.
The Philosophical Wars
The 6 Days War.
The Great War.
The Longest War.
The Never-ending War.
The War to end all Wars

The War of the Roses.
The War of the Camelias.
The War of the Hydrangeas.
The War of the Worlds.
The War of the Environment.
The War of the Planet.

Who's Wars?
Not My Wars!
No MORE Wars!
Now, that's the "Don't make me laugh" Wars.

"The Don"
10.11.2020

I Wanna Make Lo♥e with You

(Voglio Fare l'Amore Con Te)

I wanna just hold you.
No!
I wanna just hug you.
No!
I wanna just kiss you.
No!
I wanna just be with you.
No!
I wanna just see you!
No!
I wanna just sing with you.
No!
I wanna just dance with you.
No!
I wanna just make music with you.
No!
I don't wanna have sex with you.
No!
I don't wanna just FUCK you!
No!
I wanna make Lo♥e to you.
No!

I wanna make Lo♥e *WITH you.*
YES!
WITH you!
Together as one.
WITH you!
I wanna make Lo♥e *WITH you.*
Make Lo♥e *WITH you.*
WITH you!

"The Don"
10.11.2020

A Stolen Kiss
(Un Bacio Rubato)

I kiss you on the lips.
You were sleeping at the time.
You looked so innocent.
For a moment I thought you were mine.
You looked so beautiful!
So peaceful in your dreams.
I've seen this look before on you.
When you are at my place.
Listening to music that is sublime.
You seem to be transported.
To another place & time.
To exotic places that I've never been.
Of sun-drenched beaches.
And dense Amazonian Jungle.
Far away from the crazy madness.
That surrounds you all the time.
I see it in your face.
I see it in your eyes.
I feel it in your He❤rt.
I feel it in your Soul.
I feel it in your Being.
A Lo❤e so deep & profound.
It moves me to tears.
There is no "Higher ground".

But a stolen kiss.
That's all I can get.
Maybe, that's all I deserve.
But I'll take it nevertheless.
A stolen kiss is better than no kiss at all.

"The Don"
10.11.2020

Friendship Vs Relationship
(Amicizia Vs Relazione)

What is the difference between a friendship & a relationship?
Is there any difference?
When does a friendship become a relationship?
When does a relationship become a friendship?
Can you have a friendship & not be in a relationship?
Can you have a relationship & not have a friendship?
Is sex the only difference?
So, if you start fucking in your friendship it then becomes a relationship?
So, if you stop fucking in your relationship it then becomes just a friendship?
Is there a line that is crossed?
Is it an, either or situation?
Are the mutually exclusive?
Or can you have both?
Can you have a friendship & a relationship at the same time?
Can you have a relationship & a friendship at the same time?
Can you be in a friendship & a relationship?
Can they be both one & the same thing?
Can a friendship equal a relationship?

Friendship Vs Relationship

"The Don"
11.11.2020

There's Nothing More to Say
(Non c'è Altro da Dire)

I've said it all.
I've spilled out my guts.
I've opened up my He♥rt.
I've told you what's going on inside me.
I've explained my situation.
I've given you my reasons.
I've laid everything out onto the table.
I've said my piece.
I've told you where I'm at.
I've made my position clear.

You've told me your situation.
You've laid out your reasons.
You've made your position clear.

I understand that!
I now know the score.
I now know where I stand.

There's nothing more to say.

"The Don"
11.11.2020

Comfortable in Your Own Skin
(Comodo Nella tua Pelle)

Are you happy within yourself?
Are you at peace within yourself?
Are you a friend to yourself?
Are you kind to yourself?
Are you gentle to yourself?
Are you comfortable in your own skin?

Are you at conflict within yourself?
Are you at war within yourself?
Are you at battle within yourself?
Are you at odds within yourself?
Are you at rage within yourself?
Are you comfortable in your own skin?

Do you like yourself?
Do you Lo♥e yourself?
Do you care for yourself?
Do you forgive yourself?
Do you respect yourself?
Are you comfortable in your own skin?

Do you hate yourself?
Do you fight yourself?
Do you torture yourself?
Do you punish yourself?
Do you admonish yourself?
Are you comfortable in your own skin?

"The Don"
12.11.2020

It's All in Your Mind

(È Tutto Nella tua Testa)

Whatever is happening.
Whatever is going on.
Whatever is going down.
It's all in your MIND!

"I think therefore I am!"
If you can think it, it exists.
If you can dream it, it exists.
It's all in your MIND!

I see.
I hear.
I feel.
I think.
It's all in your MIND!

I plan.
I suffer.
I fear.
I Lo♥e.
It's all in your MIND!

I remember.
I desire.
I pursue.
I die.
It's all in your MIND!

I believe.
I interpret.
I imagine.
I pray.
It's all in your MIND!

Reality.
Sleep.
Spirituality
Consciousness.
It's all in your MIND!

"The Don"
13.11.2020

Life Is Not Meant to Be So Complicated

(La Vita non Dovrebbe essere così Complicata)

Things should be *easy*.
Relationships should be *easy*.
Making a living should be *easy*.
Lo♥ing someone should be *easy*.
Making Lo♥e should be *easy*.
Being friends should be *easy*.
Life should be *easy*.
Living should be *easy*.
Life is not meant to be so complicated.

Don't overthink it.
Don't over plan it.
Don't try so hard.
Don't take it so seriously.
Don't sweat it.
Don't stress it.
Don't panic.
Don't freak out.
Life is not meant to be so complicated.

Take it easy.
Take it slowly.
Take time to smell the roses.
Take a break.
Take a rest.
Take your time.
Take a breather.
Life is not meant to be so complicated.

"The Don"
13.11.2020

The War to End All Wars
(La Guerra per porre fine a tutte le Guerre)

The Great War.
The Longest War.
The 6 Days War.
The Petrol War.
The Water War.
The God War.
The Holy War.
The Unholy War.
The Legal War.
The Illegal War.
The Postponed War.
The Sanctioned War.
The Drug War.
The Religious War.
The Political War.
The Monetary War.
The Sex War.
The Power War.
The Lo♥e War.
The Gender War.
The "AI" War.
The Space War.
The Interplanetary War.
The Interstellar War.
The Futile War.
The Never-ending War.
The War to end all Wars.

"The Don"
13.11.2020

You Didn't Even Stop to Say Hello
(Non ti sei Nemmeno Fermato a Salutare)

I called out your name from the other side of the road.
You just waved at me & kept on walking.
You looked at me as if I was a stranger
It was as if you didn't even know me.
Total disconnection.

I felt it like a kick in the guts.
Like a knife was plunged into my heart.
Tears welled in my eyes.
They fell down my cheeks.
In fact, I'm cry now.
As I write these painful words.

Words of suffering.
Words of pain.
Words of loss.
Words of rejection.
Words of unrequited lo♥e.

You just kept on walking
Never looking back.
As you do.
No once do you ever look back.
You told me you would hurt me.
I said that getting hurt is part of life.
But I don't realise then, how much it would hurt.
It hurts a lot.
The suffering is unbearable.

But one thing comes out of this.
Now I know how much I really mean to you.
I mean nothing.
I don't even exist in your mind.
I don't even exist in your world.
I certainly don't exist in your he♥rt.

I shouldn't have called out!
I should've just let her keep on walking.
She had made up her mind.
She had decided.
It was my own fault.

I brought this suffering upon myself.
She is not to blame.
I made her turn around.

No long goodbyes.
No drawn out conversations.
No tedious explanations.
Here's to the Moon.
Here's to Mars.
Cheers!

Although, in hindsight,
It was to be expected.
This is what you do.
This is what you've been doing for most of your life.
How you've been living like this your whole life.
It serves you well.
Total disconnection.

Sometimes you just can't remain friends.
It's "either or!"
Either a friend.
Or a stranger.
It's one or the other!

That's the cold, hard face of reality.

"The Don"
13.11.2020

Party Animal
(Festaiolo)

You wanna PARTY?
You wanna drink?
You wanna dance?
You wanna sing?
You wanna laugh?
You wanna "Rock'n'Roll"?
You wanna have a good time?
You wanna RAGE?
You wanna make LO♥E?

You wanna get DOWN?
You wanna get HIGH?
You wanna get PLASTERED?
You wanna get WASTED?
You wanna get STONED?
You wanna get FUCKED?

You're a "Party Animal"!
So am I!
So, let's get together.
Come on over!
Let's party ALL night long.
There's NO tomorrow!
There's just NOW!
And "NOW" is "PARTY TIME"!
Party Animal!

"The Don"
14.11.2020

You Must Play Hard to Get!

(Devi Giocare Duro per Ottenere!)

You can't show that you're interested.
You can't show that you care.
You can't show too much attention.
You can't show too much affection.
You can't show too much kindness.
You can't show too much tenderness.
You can't show too much LO♥E.
You must play hard to get!

You can't be a clown.
You can't be needy.
You can't be desperate.
You can't be pathetic.
You can't be clingy.
You can't be melodramatic.
You can't be vain.
You can't be funny.
You can't be jealous.
You must play hard to get!

You gotta play it cool.
You gotta play it reserved.
You gotta play it unattainable.
You gotta play it uninterested.
You gotta play it aloof.
You gotta play it intellectual.
You must play hard to get!

You gotta play it SEXY.
You gotta play it SENSUAL.
You gotta play it with PASSION.
You gotta play it with SEXUALITY.
You must play hard to get!

"The Don"
14.11.2020

Create a Vacuum

(Crea un vuoto)

Create a space.
Create a void.
Create an emptiness.
Create a hole.
Create a longing.
Create a need.
Create a pull.
Create a force.
Create a tension.
Create a polarity.
Create a dipolar.
Create a potential.
Create an energy.
Create an attraction.
Create a vortex.
Create a Singularity.
Create a vacuum.

"The Don"
15.11.2020

The Life of an Idiot

(La Vita di un Idioto)

I talk too much.
I upset people.
I am stoopid.
I say stoopid things.
I do stoopid things.
I put my foot in my mouth.
I have a bloody big foot.
I am delusional.
I am irrational.
I daydream.
I romanticise.
I fantansise.
I am jealous.
I am needy.
I am impulsive.
I don't focus.
I let my emotions rule me.
I have no willpower.
I am weak.
I don't know when to stop.
I don't know when to "back off".
I'm a "try hard".
I'm not serious enough.
I joke around too much.
I am pathetic.
I am a loser.
I am crazy.
I'm a fool.
I'm not normal.
I am an IDIOT!

"The Don"
17.11.2020

Cunt

(is not a dirty word)
Fica (non è una sporca parola)

Don't you believe what you've seen or you've heard.
Cunt (is not a dirty word).
Don't shudder when you the word.
Cunt (is not a dirty word).
Don't see it a disgusting.
Cunt (is not a dirty word).
Don't see as repulsive.
Cunt (is not a dirty word).
Don't use it to degrade.
Cunt (is not a dirty word).
Don't use it to abuse.
Cunt (is not a dirty word).
Don't use it to put someone down.
Cunt (is not a dirty word).
Don't use it as a swear word.
Cunt (is not a dirty word).
Don't perpetuate derogatory use.
Cunt (is not a dirty word).

Cunt is a beautiful word.
Cunt (is not a dirty word).
Cunt is about femininity.
Cunt (is not a dirty word).
Cunt is about womanhood.
Cunt (is not a dirty word).

Cunt is about sisterhood.
Cunt (is not a dirty word).
Cunt is about power.
Cunt (is not a dirty word).
Cunt is about birth.
Cunt (is not a dirty word).
Cunt is a thing of beauty.
Cunt (is not a dirty word).
Cunt is about LO♥E.
Cunt (is not a dirty word).

Be a CUNT!
Because Cunt (is not a dirty word).
Shout it out loud!
Cunt (is not a dirty word).
"I am a cunt & " I am proud!"
Cunt (is not a dirty word).

Don't you believe what you've seen or you've heard.
Cunt (is not a dirty word).

Cunt (is not a dirty word).

Cunt (is not a dirty word).

Cunt (is not a dirty word).

Cunt (is not a dirty word).

"The Don"
17.11.2020

Everybody's So Fucking Boring
(Sono tutti così Fottutamente Noiosi)

Not interested in art?
Not interested in films?
Not interested in history?
Not interested in music?
Not interested in politics?
Not interested in science?
Not interested in technology?
Not interested in sport?
Not interested in social issues?
Not interested in culture?
Not interested in dancing?
Not interested in singing?
Not interested in environmental issues?
Not interested in social equality?
Not interested in redistribution of wealth?
Not interested in world events?
You're so fucking boring.

Don't know anything about music?
Don't know anything about art?
Don't know anything about science?
Don't know anything about philosophy?
Don't know anything about history?
Don't know anything about architecture?
Don't know anything about politics?
Don't know anything about world events?
Don't know anything about political philosophy?
Don't know anything about economics?
Don't know anything about literature?
Don't know anything about culture?
Don't know anything about creativity?
Don't know anything about passion?
Don't know anything about desire?
Don't know anything about LO♥E?
You are one boring fuck!

Interested in making money?
Interested in climbing the corporate ladder?
Interested in acquiring material possessions?
Interested in social prestige?
Interested in appearances?
Interested in Capitalism?
Interested in "Popularism"?
Interested in conforming?
Interested in conformity?
Interested in being "normal"?
Interested in uniformity?
Interested in nationalism?
Interested in militarism?
Interested in monopolies?
Interested in competition?
Interested in being competitive?
Interested in control?
Interested in controlling?
Interested in power?
You're so fucking boring.

Everybody's so fucking boring!

Except YOU!
And me, of course!

"The Don"
17.11.2020

The waiting Game

(Il Gioco in Attesa)

Sometimes you've just gotta bide your time.
Sometimes things don't work out smoothly.
Sometimes events seem to conspire against you.
Sometimes things don't work out your way.
Sometimes things take longer to come together.
Sometimes it's just a waiting game.
Sometimes that's all there is to it.
Sometimes you've just gotta wait.

Sometimes there is nothing you can do.
Sometimes you can't push things along.
Sometimes you can't force things to an end.
Sometimes you've just gotta be patient.
Sometimes you've just gotta hang on.
Sometimes you've just gotta have faith.
Sometimes you've just gotta trust Destiny.
Sometimes you've just gotta wait.
Sometimes that's all there is to it.
Sometimes you've just gotta wait.

"The waiting is the hardest part.
Every day you get one more yard.
You take it on faith, you take it to the heart.
The waiting is the hardest part.
Yeah, the waiting is the hardest part."

"The Waiting" written by Tom Petty

"The Don"
17.11.2020

Nothing Ever Happens the Way You Want It To
(Non Succede Mai Niente nel Modo in cui lo Desideri)

You gotta a plan?
You gotta a strategy?
You gotta a scheme?
You gotta a need?
Nothing ever happens the way you want it to.

Expect changes of plans.
Expect cancellations.
Expect unexpected rearrangements.
Expect the unexpected.
Because, nothing ever happens the way you want it to.

Be flexible.
Be accommodating.
Be loose.
Be free.
Be fluidic.
Nothing ever happens the way you want it to.

Go with the flow.
Go with the energy.
Go with the evolution of things.
Go with Karma.
Nothing ever happens the way you want it to.

Don't panic.
Don't stress.
Don't fret.
Don't get scared.
Nothing ever happens the way you want it to.

"The Don"
17.11.2020

I Know Nothing

(Io non so Nulla)

I have no ideas.
I have no plans.
I have no thoughts.
I have no imagination.
I have no opinions.
I have no interests.
I have no skills.
I have no knowledge.
I have no education.
I have no pursuits.
I have no ambition.
I have no motivation.
I have no religion.
I have no spirituality.
I have no insights.
I have no foresight.
I have no hindsight.
I have no sight.
I have no eyes.
I have no ears.
I have no mouth.
I have no creativity.
I have no consciousness.
I have no brain.
I have no mind.

I know nothing.
I know that, I know nothing.

"The Don"
17.11.2020

Honesty is the Best Policy

(L'onestà è la Miglior Politica)

Be honest.
Tell the truth.
Don't hide behind a lie.
Tell it as it is.
Have a clear conscience.
Have a clear mind.
Sleep well at night.

Nothing good comes from a lie.
Only falsehoods can be built upon lies.
Maintaining a lie is difficult.
Remembering your last lie is hard.
You will be found out in the end.
Your tangled web of deceit will eventually unravel.
Your facade of lies will fall down.
And you will be exposed for the fraud that you are.
You will stand naked for everyone to see who you really are.

A fake & a fraud.
A liar.
With nowhere to hide.
Exposed for all the world to see.
Exposed.
Denuded.
Unmasked.
Pilloried.
Ridiculed.
Embarrassed.
Shamed.
Alone.
Abandoned
Crucified.
Hung out to dry.
Eaten by maggots.

Honesty is the best policy.

"The Don"
17.11.2020

Partners in Crime

(Complici nel Crimine)

Batman & Robin.
Bonnie & Clyde.
Dean Martin & Jerry Lewis.
Abbott & Costello.
The Lone Ranger & Tonto.
Ren & Stympie.
Fred Astaire & Ginger Rogers.
Superboy & Krypto.
The Captain & Tennile.
Simon & Garfunkel.
Sonny & Cher.
Bob Dylan & The Band.
Ronnie Hawkins & The Hawks.
Buddy Holly & The Crickets.
Tom Petty & The Heartbreakers.
Johnny Diesel & The Injectors.
Paul Kelly & The Coloured Balls.
Eric Burdon & The Animals
Syd & Nancy.
Elizabeth Taylor & Richard Burton.
Antony & Cleopatra.
Sampson & Delilah.
Sodom & Gomorrah.
Willy & The Handjive.
George Thoroughgood & The Destroyers.
Bill Haley & The Comets.
Victoria & Albert.
Dolce & Gabbana.
Gilbert & Sullivan.
Romulus & Remus.
Venus & Mars.
John & Yoko.
Bill & Tony.
Oli & Popeye.
Frankie Lee & Judas Priest.
Butch Cassidy & the Sundance Kid.
Miriam & "The Don".
Cheech & Chong.
Chicco Chicci & Franchi Ingrassi.

Who is your partner in crime?

"The Don"
19.11.2020

You Talk a Lot for Someone with Nothing to Say
(Parli Molto per Qualcuno che non ha Niente da Dire)

For someone with no brain.
You have a lot to say.
For someone with no mind.
You have a lot to say.
For someone with no mouth.
You have a lot to say.
For someone with no tongue.
You have a lot to say.
For someone with no ears.
You have a lot to say.
For someone with no eyes.
You have a lot to say.
For someone with no thoughts.
You have a lot to say.
For someone with no ideas.
You have a lot to say.
For someone with no interests.
You have a lot to say.
For someone with no motivation.
You have a lot to say.
For someone with no inspiration.
You have a lot to say.
For someone with no Desires.
You have a lot to say.
For someone with no Passion.
You have a lot to say.
For someone with no Life.
You have a lot to say.
For someone with no Spirituality.
You have a lot to say.
For someone with no Being.
You have a lot to say.

You sure have a lot to say!
For someone with nothing to say!

"The Don"
19.11.2020

Birthday

(Compleanno)

Birth day.
Day of your birth.
Day when you entered this planet.
First day of your existence.
First day of you your first breath.
First cry.
First day of opening your eyes.
First of opening your mouth.
First time you sucked on your mother's nipple.
First time you swallowed.
First time you were held in human arms.
First time you were kissed.
First time you smiled.
First time you laughed.
First time you pooed.
First time you held another human's hand.
First time you saw another human's face.
First time you felt LO♥E.

Let's celebrate the "first day of your life".
Let's celebrate the "Day of your Birth".
Let's celebrate your "Birth Day".
Let's celebrate the "most important day of your life".
Let's celebrate your "Birthday".

"You say it's your birthday
It's my birthday too, yeah
They say it's your birthday
We're gonna have a good time
I'm glad it's your birthday
Happy birthday to you

Yes, we're going to a party party
Yes, we're going to a party party
Yes, we're going to a party party
I would like you to dance, birthday
Take a cha-cha-cha-chance, birthday
I would like you to dance, birthday Dance

I would like you to dance, birthday
Take a cha-cha-cha-chance, birthday
I would like you to dance, birthday Dance

You say it's your birthday
Well, it's my birthday too, yeah
You say it's your birthday
We're gonna have a good time
I'm glad it's your birthday
Happy birthday to you."

Songwriters: John Lennon / Paul McCartney

"Happy birthday to you
Happy birthday to you
Happy birthday dear my friend
Happy birthday to you

You're waking up another year has come to you
To celebrate this day with you
Don't I have to be anymore there way toward now
'Cause, I can never thank enough for you to stay up here in my life
So, make a wish out loud see if you can make it through
You know that I'll be there when you need me

Happy birthday to you
Happy birthday to you
Happy birthday dear my friend
Happy birthday to you

And away we're here wishing all the shining stars
Thank you and you're my loved one
I'm having and a lot

Happy birthday to you
Happy birthday to you
Happy birthday dear my friend
Happy birthday to you."

Songwriter: Wonder Stevie

"The Don"
22.11.2020

Throw Caution to the Wind
(Getta Cautela al Vento)

Don't be cautious.
Don't be scared.
Don't be afraid.
Don't live in fear.
Throw caution to the wind.

Take risks.
Be adventurous.
Walk on the "wild side".
Experience.
Experiment.
Enjoy.
Have FUN.
Throw caution to the wind.

Be courageous.
Be strong.
Be wild.
Be crazy.
Be beautiful.
Be happy.
Have FUN.
Throw caution to the wind.

Live your life!
Don't throw it away.
Don't waste it.
Don't wait for tomorrow.
Don't make excuses.
Don't delay.
Start today.
This VERY moment.
Throw caution to the wind.

"Dedicated to my friend "Molly" from "Tom-Yum Tum-Gang" in Glebe. She just works & sleeps. She has NO life!"

"The Don"
22.11.2020

You Can't Be Everything to One Person
(Non Puoi essere tutto per una Persona)

You cannot satisfy one person's every need.
You cannot satisfy one person's every desire.
You've got to understand that there are some things that you cannot give.
You've got to accept that there are some things you do not have.
You've gotta to understand these will be met by someone else.
You've got to understand that these will be fulfilled by another.
You Can't Be Everything to One Person.

This also true for you.
Don't expect one person to fulfill all your needs.
Don't place these sort of demands upon them.
You will only be disappointed.
You will only create discord.
You will only create false expectations.
You will only live with false hope.
You Can't Be Everything to One Person.

Accept there will be many people in your life.
Accept that there will be many people in everyone else's life.
That you are only a part of their lives.
That you are only a part of their world.
You will move in & out.
As they will move in & out of yours.
Allow this movement to occur freely.
Do NOT put obstacles in the way.
Do NOT put barriers in the way.
Do NOT put a blockage in the way.
Do NOT shut the way.
ALWAYS keep it open.
This is the ONLY way!
You Can't Be Everything to One Person.

"The Don"
22.11.2020

People Take Life Too Seriously

(Le Persone Prendono la Vita Troppo sul Serio)

Lighten up.
Have FUN.
Muck around.
Fool around.
People take life too seriously.

Life's a joke.
You are born & then you die.
What's it all for?
Absolutely NOTHING!
People take life too seriously.

You struggle all of your life.
That thing in between being born & dying.
What's it all for?
It's a joke.
People take life too seriously.

There's no point in life.
It just is.
There is no higher purpose.
There is no meaning.
People take life too seriously.

Life just IS.
Life just happens.
And Life happened to you.
That's all there is to it.
People take life too seriously.

Don't make it more than what it is.
Don't take it so seriously.
It's just a waste of your time.
It's just a waste of your energy.
People take life too seriously.

Don't take life too seriously.

"The Don"
22.11.2020

Empty Chair

(Sedia Vuota)

Who was sitting there?
It looks so lonely.
It looks so sad.
Was it meant for someone?
Is it waiting for someone?
Empty chair.

Who has sat on it?
What stories it can tell.
Sad tales of unrequited LO♥E.
Sadder tales of jilted LO♥E.
Saddest tales of rejected LO♥E.
Oh, *Empty chair.*

It has seen tears.
It has heard laughter.
It has felt sadness.
It has felt loss.
It has experienced LO♥E.
This *Empty chair.*

Tonight, it is empty.
There is no laughter.
There is no singing.
There is no fun.
There is no LO♥E.
Sad *Empty chair.*

But do not despair.
There is music in the air.
The music will NEVER die.
Nick Cave won't let it.
This lonely, *Empty chair.*

He will let your Spirit fly.
He will take you to Heaven.
He will raise you to your feet.
He will move you beyond the mundane.
He will speak directly to your HEART.
He will sleep with you Soul.
You will feel protected in his arms.
He will not let anyone harm you.
He will gently cradle you like a mother.
Like a LOVER.
He whispers a lullaby into your ears.
He will gently caress your cheeks.
He will lightly kiss your lips.
He will gently put you to sleep.
You are happy in his arms.
Oh, *Empty chair.*

Will it ever be filled?
Maybe, it will always remain empty.
Never to experience the warmth of a human again.
Never to be needed again.
Never to be sat on again.
Never to be included again.
Never to experience again.
Oh, *Empty chair.*

Will your call be heard?
Will your call be answered?
Will you see her again?
The one who you LOVE so deeply.
You allow her to sit on you.
You give yourself to her.
So completely.
She will return.
Of that I am sure.
No longer, an *Empty chair.*

"I feel the trembling tingle of a sleepless night
Creep through my fingers and the moon is bright
Beams of blue come flickering through my window pane
Like gypsy moths that dance around a candle flame.

And I wonder if you know
That I never understood
That although you said you'd go
Until you did, I never thought you would.

Moonlight used to bathe the contours of your face
While chestnut hair fell all around the pillow case
And the fragrance of your flowers rest beneath my head
A sympathy bouquet left with the love that's dead.

And I wonder if you know
That I never understood
That although you said you'd go
Until you did, I never thought you would.

Never thought the words you said were true
Never thought you said just what you meant
Never knew how much I needed you
Never thought you'd leave, until you went.

Morning comes and morning goes with no regret
And evening brings the memories I can't forget
Empty rooms that echo as I climb the stairs
And empty clothes that drape and fall on empty chairs.

And I wonder if you know
That I never understood
That although you said you'd go
Until you did, I never thought you would."

Songwriter: Don Mclean

"The Don"
22.11.2020

Photo taken by "The Don"

I Am TOO Loud

(Sono TROPPO Rumoroso)

I am loud.
That is true!
But am I TOO Loud?
In my defence.
I am Italian.
We are notoriously known for being LOUD.
That is part of our culture.
It's part of our Nature.
It's who we are.
We are loud.
But are we TOO loud?

We get too excited.
We have to gesticulate with our arms.
Our mouths aren't big enough.
Our voice is not loud enough.
It cannot convey the whole story.
Things need to be said.
A picture has to be painted.
The story must be told.
The story must be heard.
VERY LOUD!

When I was born, I came with instructions.
"Must be played VERY LOUD!"
There is no other way.
It's either volume set to 12.
Or nothing at all.
There is NO middle ground.
There is no range.
From zero to 10.
There is only one setting.
It's ALWAYS set to MAXIMUM.
ELEVEN!
VERY LOUD!

That's the way it is with me.
I've been told to tone it down.
Ivy been told to turn it down.
I've been told I'm TOO loud.
I've heard it many times.
I've heard it all my life.
It's not something new.
"You are VERY loud!"

There's nothing I can do about it.
It's in my DNA.
That's what people don't understand.
That's who I am.
I am VERY loud!
It can put a lot of people off.
Believe me it has.
People have called me "obnoxious".
People have called me "arrogant".
Because I am VERY loud!

I didn't choose to be born this way.
FUCK, I didn't choose to be born at all.
I was never given a say in the matter.
There was no round table conversation.
There was no quiet invitation.
There was no asking my permission.
There was no consideration given to my interest in the matter.
There was no formal request presented.
"Do you wish to be born?"
"VERY LOUD?"

Anyway, how loud is "TOO loud?"

I think that it was just my laugh that was loud.
I have a very HEARTY laugh.

"The Don"
23.11.2020

I Can Be Quiet

(Posso Stare Tranquillo)

I can keep my mouth shut.
I can stop talking.
I can be silent.
I can be quiet!

I can hear the "Sound of Silence".
I can listen to the gentle song of the breeze.
I can become one with "Nature".
I can be quiet!

I can sit & meditate.
I can listen to your HEART beat.
I can hear your HEART beating.
I can be quiet!

I can see your suffering.
I can hear your suffering.
I can feel your suffering.
I can be quiet!

Let me share it with you.
Let me be a shoulder for you to rest your head upon
Let me in.
I can be quiet!

Don't shut me out.
Don't keep me out.
Don't close the door upon me.
I can be quiet!

"The Don"
23.11.2020

Time Heals All Wounds

(Il Tempo Guarisce Tutte le Ferite)

Time heals all wounds.
Of that I am certain.
It's happened many times before.
But it never gets any easier.
The suffering is intense.
The pain is raw.
The HEART has been damaged.
Hopefully, not irreparably.
A knife has been plunged deep into your gut.
You are finding it difficult to breathe.
You have been winded.
You have been left breathless.
You have been left stranded.
You have been abandoned.
You have been rejected.
You have fallen to your knees.
Your head is spinning around.
Your mind is in a state of chaos.
You're in the "State of Confusion".
Tears well up on your eyes.
They fall down your face.
Like a waterfall, they flow down your cheeks.
Down over your lips.
You taste their salty sadness.
The taste of sadness.
You have tasted them before.
It brings back painful memories.
You just let them flow.
There is no need to stop the flow.
They will stop when they are ready.
You put your head on your pillow.
You lay your head down to rest.
Time heals all wounds.
And it will heal this wound too.
....in time!

"The Don"
23.11.2020

My World

(Il Mio Mondo)

My World is full of *MUSIC*.
My World is full of *SINGING*.
My World is full of *DANCING*.
My World is full of *LAUGHTER*.
My World is full of *RAUCOUS LAUGHTER*.
My World is full of *FUN*.
My World is full of *HAPPINESS*.
My World is full of *POSITIVITY*.
My World is full of *JOY*.
My World is full of *HOPE*.
My World is full of *HILARITY*.
My World is full of getting *HIGH*.
My World is full of *STRENGTH*.
My World is full of *COURAGE*.
My World is full of *ADVENTURE*.
My World is full of *LIFE*.
My World is full of *PASSION*.
My World is full of *DESIRE*.
My World is full of *BEAUTY*.
My World is full of *STRENGTH*.
My World is full of *RESILIENCE*.
My World is full of *RESPECT*.
My World is full of *COMPASSION*.
My World is full of *FRIENDSHIP*.
My World is full of *SOUL*.
My World is full of *LOVE*.
My World is full of *HEART*.

My World sometimes has *SADNESS*.
My World sometimes has *TEARS*.
My World sometimes has *FEAR*.
My World sometimes has *JEALOUSY*.
My World sometimes has *SUFFERING*.
My World sometimes has *DOUBTS*.
From rejected LOVE.

How is YOUR World?
What is it full of?

"The Don"
24.11.2020

Time

(Tempo)

Time marches on.
Time is relentless.
Time NEVER stops.
Time NEVER slows down.
Time doesn't wait for anyone.
Time continues on forward path.
Time takes everything with it.
Time spares no one.
Time spares nothing.
Time marches forward on its lonely journey.
Time has no friends.
Time doesn't need any!
Time doesn't need any one!
Time doesn't need anything!
Time is CRUEL!
Time is illusive.
Time cannot be captured.
Time cannot be slowed down.
Time cannot be stopped.
Time cannot be reversed.
Time only goes in one direction, FORWARD.
Time has no purpose.
Time has no meaning.
Time has no reasoning.
Time has no being.
Time has no HEART.
Time has no Soul.
Time is NOTHING.
Time doesn't even EXIST.

"The Don"
24.11.2020

Use It or Lose it

(Usalo o Perdi)

Your *eyes*.
Use it or lose it.
Your *ears*.
Use it or lose it.
Your *mouth*.
Use it or lose it.
Your *sensuality*.
Use it or lose it.
Your *sexuality*.
Use it or lose it.
Your *sex*.
Use it or lose it.
Your *pussy*.
Use it or lose it.
Your *clit*.
Use it or lose it.
Your *cock*.
Use it or lose it.
Your *brain*.
Use it or lose it.
Your *mind*.
Use it or lose it.
Your *creativity*.
Use it or lose it.
Your *Soul*.
Use it or lose it.
Your *HEART*.
Use it or lose it.
Your *LOVE*.
Use it or lose it.
Your *BEING*.
Use it or lose it.
Your *SPIRITUALITY*.
Use it or lose it.
Your *HUMANITY*.
Use it or lose it.
Use it or lose it.
Use it or lose it.
Use it or lose it.

"The Don"
26.11.2020

Tinder Surprise (Kinder for Adults)

Tinder Surprise (Kinder per Adulti)

What will you find in your next "Tinder Surprise" (Kinder for adults)?

A long & prosperous life.
Happiness ever after.
Eternal youth.
A facelift.
A smile.
Eyes.
Ears.
A mouth.
A tongue.
A brain.
A Mind.
A Soul.
A HEART.
Humanity.
Kindness.
Compassion.
Humour.
Intelligence.
Empathy.
Respect.

A "playmate".
A "Soulmate".

How about a free brain transplant?
A new political system?
Universal health care for everyone?
$1 million?
A woman president in Brazil?
A woman president in the USA?
An African American president in the USA?

We can only DREAM?

What will you find in your next "Tinder Surprise" (Kinder for adults)?

"The Don"
27.11.2020

Everything Has A Price
(You're gonna have to pay somebody!)

Tutto ha un Prezzo (Dovrai Pagare Qualcuno!)

You're gonna have to pay somebody!
Wanna be my FRIEND?
You're gonna have to pay somebody!
Wanna have some FUN?
You're gonna have to pay somebody!
Wanna take me out on a DATE?
You're gonna have to pay somebody!
Wanna IMPRESS me?
You're gonna have to pay somebody!
Wanna HOLD me?
You're gonna have to pay somebody!
Wanna HUG me?
You're gonna have to pay somebody!
Wanna TOUCH me THERE?
You're gonna have to pay somebody!
Wanna KISS me?
You're gonna have to pay somebody!
Want me to stay the NIGHT?
You're gonna have to pay somebody!
Wanna take me to BED?
You're gonna have to pay somebody!
Wanna SLEEP with me?
You're gonna have to pay somebody!
Wanna have SEX!
You're gonna have to pay somebody!
Wanna FUCK?
You're gonna have to pay somebody!
Wanna make LOVE?
You're gonna have to pay somebody!
Wanna have my HEART?
You're gonna have to pay somebody!
Wanna have my SOUL?
You're gonna have to pay somebody!
Want my BEING?
You're gonna have to pay somebody!
"Well, it may be the Devil or it may be the Lord.
But you're gonna have pay somebody!"

"The Don"
30.11.2020

Power is Evil

(Il Potere è Male)

It's a dirty word.
Everyone wants it.
Whether you realise it or not.
Life is ALL about POWER.
Who has it!
Who protects it!
Who hasn't got it!
Who wants it!

If you have POWER.
You don't want to lose it.
You don't want to give it away.
If you don't have POWER.
You want it.
You'll do ANYTHING to get it.

It's in relationships.
It's in families.
It's in friendships.
It's in the work place.
It's in the church.
It's in politics.
It's in society.

Everything is about POWER.
POWER over yourself.
POWER over others.
POWER over other countries.
POWER to CONTROL.
POWER to get others to do what you want.
POWER as entertainment.
POWER as greed.
POWER as pleasure.
POWER as a DRUG!
POWER is systemic.
POWER is endemic.
POWER is pathetic.

POWER is arrogant.
POWER is addictive.
POWER is destructive.
POWER is corruptive.
POWER is insidious.
POWER is corrosive.
POWER is hatred.
POWER is Evil.

"The Don"
01.12.2020

Time Heals All Wounds (Hurt)
(Il Tempo Guarisce tutte le Ferite (Ferite))

Time heals all wounds.......
.......or so it is said.
But does it really?
Are there some wounds that can never be healed?
No matter how much time passes?
No matter how long you wait?

If it hasn't healed, then not enough time has passed....
.......it is also said.
But is this true?
Are there some wounds that can never be healed?
No matter how much time passes?
No matter how long you wait?

Healing is a funny thing.
Forgiving is a funny thing.
Forgiveness is a funny thing.
LOVE is a funny thing.

Sometimes we hurt others & we don't even know it.
Sometimes we just take things too far.
Sometimes we cross the line without knowing it.
Sometimes we don't even know there was a line to cross.
Sometimes we are just too blind to see.
Sometimes we just don't want to see.
Sometimes we are too deaf to hear.
Sometimes we just don't want to hear.
Sometimes we just don't want to get hurt.
Sometimes we just want to hurt.
Sometimes we just want LOVE.
Sometimes we just want to feel.
Sometimes we just want.

"I hurt myself today
To see if I still feel
I focus on the pain
The only thing that's real.

The needle tears a hole
The old familiar sting
Try to kill it all away
But I remember everything.

What have I become?
My sweetest friend?
Everyone I know
Goes away in the end.

And you could have it all
My empire of dirt
I will let you down
I will make you hurt.

I wear this crown of thorns
Upon my liar's chair
Full of broken thoughts
I cannot repair.

Beneath the stains of time
The feelings disappear
You are someone else
I am still right here.

What have I become?
My sweetest friend?
Everyone I know
Goes away in the end.

And you could have it all
My empire of dirt
I will let you down
I will make you hurt.

If I could start again
A million miles away
I will keep myself
I would find a way."

Songwriter: Trent Reznor

"The Don"
01.12.2020

Soulmate (& Myself)

Anima Gemella (e Me Stesso)

I have never felt like this before about someone.
I have heard of this but, I never really believed in it.
Until I met you.
Now, I understand.
Now, I feel it.
You are my *"Soulmate"*.

I feel you in my gut.
I can't stop thinking about you.
I try to get you of my head.
But I just can't!
When I don't see you for a few days it's as though my gut has been wrenched out.
Torn out.
I feel sick in my stomach.
I feel nauseous.
This can't be normal?
This is ridiculous.
For a 61 year young man to feel like this!

I tell myself to grow up.
I tell myself to stop acting like a LOVE sick puppy.
I tell myself to get it together.
I tell myself to get a grip.
I tell myself to get over it.
I tell myself all sorts of things.
I tell myself.
I tell myself.
I tell myself.
I tell myself.

But.......
Myself doesn't listen.
Myself is deaf.
Myself doesn't want to hear.
Myself is obstinate.
Myself is *"hard-headed"*.
Myself is a stubborn ol' bastard.
Myself refuses to do what it's told.

Myself continues on with its delusions.
Myself continues maintaining its fantasies.
Myself doesn't care.
Myself throws logic out the window.
Myself throws reason to the wind.
Myself is a romantic.
Myself sees logic & laughs in its face.

What can I do with "Myself"?

"The Don"
01.12.2020

Energy

(Energia)

The more you do
The more energy you have.
It's a conundrum.
It's a paradox.
It seems wrong.
Logic seems to suggest the opposite.
The less you do
The more energy you should have.
The idea of " Conservation of Energy".

But this is wrong.
On the contrary.

The more you do.
The more energy you generate.
It's a mental thing!
It's all in the head.
It's all in your mind.

It has to do with enthusiasm.
It has to do with inspiration.
It has to do with motivation.
It has to do with positivity.
It has to do with reception of energy.
It has to do with new experiences.
It has to do with new positive experiences.
It has to do with new perceptions.
It has to do with new ways of seeing things.
It has to do with chemistry.
It has to do with cells in the body producing energy.
It has to do with "The Light"!
It has to do with "The Force"!
It has to do with "The LIFE Force"!
It has to do with being ALIVE!
It has to do with LIVING!

NOT just EXISTING!

"The Don"
02.12.2020

Don't Get Married

(Non Sposarti)

You're not an object to be bought & sold.
You're not a commodity.
You're not a play thing.
You're not a servant.
You're not a slave.
You're not a sex toy.
You're not a domestic worker.
You're not a baby producing machine.
You're not a mother.
You're not a father.
You're not a provider.
You're not a security blanket.
You're not a rag.
You're not a bag.
You're not a disposable item.
You're not a punching bag.
You're not a brick wall.
You're not a THING.

You are not a NOTHING!

You're a HUMAN BEING!
You deserve KINDNESS.
You deserve DIGNITY.
You deserve RESPECT.
You deserve HUMANITY.
You deserve LOVE.

So, don't get married!

"The Don"
02.12.2020

Born to DIE!

(Nato per Morire!)

Born to DIE!
Born to DIE!
Born to DIE!
Born to DIE!
Born to DIE!
Born to DIE!
Born to DIE!
Born to DIE!
Born to DIE!
Born to DIE!
Born to DIE!
Born to DIE!
Born to DIE!
Born to DIE!
Born to DIE!
Born to DIE!

We are Born to DIE!

"The Don"
02.12.2020

You're Having TOO MUCH FUN!!

(Ti Stai Divertendo TROPPO !!)

You're Having TOO MUCH FUN!!!!!!!!!
You're Having TOO MUCH FUN!!!!!!!!!
You're Having TOO MUCH FUN!!!!!!!!!
You're Having TOO MUCH FUN!!!!!!!!!
You're Having TOO MUCH FUN!!!!!!!!!
You're Having TOO MUCH FUN!!!!!!!!!
You're Having TOO MUCH FUN!!!!!!!!!
You're Having TOO MUCH FUN!!!!!!!!!
TOO MUCH FUN!!!!!!!!!!
TOO MUCH FUN!!!!!!!!!!
TOO MUCH FUN!!!!!!!!!!
TOO MUCH FUN!!!!!!!!!!
TOO MUCH FUN!!!!!!!!!!
TOO MUCH FUN!!!!!!!!!!
TOO MUCH FUN!!!!!!!!!!
TOO MUCH FUN!!!!!!!!!!
FUN!!!!!!!!!
FUN!!!!!!!!!
FUN!!!!!!!!!
FUN!!!!!!!!!
FUN!!!!!!!!!
FUN!!!!!!!!!
FUN!!!!!!!!!
FUN!!!!!!!!!

STOP!!!!!!!!!!!!!!!!!!!!!!!!!!!!!!!!

"The Don"
02.12.2020

I'm Selfish

(Io sono Egoisto)

I like to *give*.
I LO♥E to *give*.
I like to *laugh*.
I LO♥E to *laugh*.
I like *laughter*.
I LO♥E *laughter*.
I like to *socialise*.
I LO♥E to *socialise*.
I like *people*.
I LO♥E *people*.
I like to have *FUN*.
I LO♥E to have *FUN*.
I like to *sing*.
I LO♥E to *sing*.
I like to *dance*.
I LO♥E to *dance*.
I like *music*.
I LO♥E *music*.
I like to play *music*.
I LO♥E to play *music*.
I like to get *HIGH*.
I LO♥E to get *HIGH*.
I like to *cuddle*.
I LO♥E to *cuddle*.
I like to *hug*.
I LO♥E to *hug*.
I like to *kiss*.
I LO♥E to *kiss*.
I like to make *LO♥E*.
I LO♥E to make *LO♥E*.

I'm *selfish*!
I'm soooooooooooo *selfish*.
I ONLY think about myself!

"The Don"
03.12.2020

I Stared into the Faces of Death

(Fissai i Facce della Morte)

I looked around me.
I looked about me.
I looked at their faces.
I looked at each of them.
I looked into their faces one by one.
I looked & was saddened.
I looked & was shocked.
I looked for a sign.
I looked for any sign.
I looked for a spark.
I looked for a flame.
I looked for a light.
I looked for a smile.
I looked for vitality.
I looked for energy.
I looked to find anything.
I looked & found nothing in their faces.
I looked & saw nothing in their eyes.

I looked in astonishment.
I looked in amazement.
I looked in horror.

I looked & saw boredom in their faces.
I looked & saw boredom in their eyes.
I looked & saw "Black Holes" in their faces.
I looked & saw "Black Holes" in their eyes.
I looked & found nothing in their faces.
I looked & just saw the cold, hard look of emptiness.
I looked & just saw the cold, hard look of emptiness in their faces.
I looked & just saw the cold, hard look of emptiness in their eyes.
I looked & saw no *LIFE* in their faces.
I looked & saw no *LIFE* in their eyes.
I looked & saw no *LIFE* at all.
I looked & saw *DEATH* in their faces.
I looked & saw *DEATH* in their eyes.
I looked & stared into the faces of *DEATH*.

I stood up & walked outside.
I stood up & walked outside into the rain.
I walked outside into the rain & found *LIFE*.

"The Don"
06.12.2020

The Club of Rome

(Il Club di Roma)

It's a secret Society.
Its members are intellectuals.
You can join by invitation only.
They will find you.
You cannot find them.
It's The Club of Rome.

Its meetings are secret.
They meet in secret.
No one knows who its members are.
No one knows how many members there are.
You cannot refuse its invitation.
When The Club of Rome comes calling.

Its agenda is a secret.
Its purpose unknown.
It has existed since ancient times.
There are many stories of its existence.
There are many myths surrounding its purpose.
Nobody knows what the truth is, about The Club of Rome.

I have my own ideas.
It's a society about "Ideas".
Its purpose, to keep "Ideas" alive.
In a world where "Ideas" are scorned.
In a world where "Thinkers" are ridiculed.
The Club of Rome is their home.

Its members come from all walks of life.
There are scientists, poets, philosophers, mathematicians, cosmologist & scholars.
They are equal numbers of men & women.
They meet to save Humanity.
They are the "Doomsday Vault" of "Thinkers".
They are the "Future" of Humanity.
This is, The Club of Rome.

It is the keeper of "Thought".
It is the keeper of "The Light".
It will protect "Ideas".
It will emerge when the World is ready.
Today is not it's time.
Today's world is the "Death of Thought".
Today's world is the "Death of Thinking".
Today's world is the "World of Stupidity".
Today's world is the "World of Idiocy".
Today's world is a "World in crisis".
Today's world is not a place, for The Club of Rome.

"The Don"
08.12.2020

Books written by "The Don"

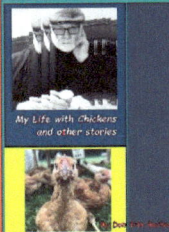
"My Life with Chickens & other stories: I Pity the Poor Immigrant"
Published:
10th September, 2019
Autobiography Book 1:
0 – 12 years old

"Poems for Misfits, Miscreants, Misanthropes, Mavericks, Losers & Malcontents!"
Published:
10th June, 2020
Book of Poems 1

"Poems for Troubled Minds & Trouble Hearts"
Published:
10th August, 2020
Book of Poems 2

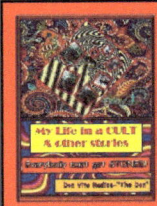
"My Life in a CULT & other stories: Everybody Must Get STONED!"
Published:
10th September, 2020
Autobiography Book 2:
15 – 30 years old

"Poems for Restless Minds & Restless Hearts"
Published:
10th October, 2020
Book of Poems 3

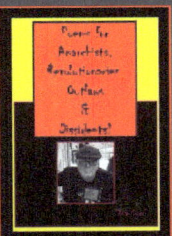
"Poems for Anarchists, Revolutionaries, Outlaws & Dissidents!"
Published:
10th November, 2020
Book of Poems 4

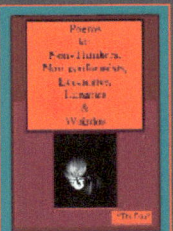
"Poems for Non-Thinkers & Eccentrics"
Published:
10th December, 2020
Book of Poems 5

"The Rantings of a Madman"
Published:
10th January, 2021
Book of Poems 6

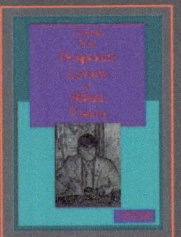
"Poems for Desperate Lovers & Silent Voices"
Published:
10th February, 2021
Book of Poems 7

"Poems for Tormented Minds & Tortured Souls"
Published:
10th March, 2021
Book of Poems 8

All available ONLY online

Books written by "The Don"

"Poems for ALIENS, Outsiders, Outcasts & other STRANGE BEINGS!"
Published: 10th April, 2021
Book of Poems 9

"Poems for Beings From Another Planet"
Published: 10th May, 2021
Book of Poems 10

All available ONLY online

Vito Radice ("The Don"):
Poet/Author/Polemicist/Non-Thinker/Non-Intellectual
To get in touch with "The Don":
Email: donvito7070@gmail.com
Instagram: don_vito_radice
Facebook: Don Vito Radice
Mobile: +61490012461 (Australia)

www.ingramcontent.com/pod-product-compliance
Lightning Source LLC
Chambersburg PA
CBHW041502010526
44107CB00049B/1625